Photography in the Twentieth Century

By Nathan Lyons

Photography in the Twentieth Century

Horizon Press, New York,

in collaboration with

The George Eastman House,

Rochester, New York.

This current book was prepared by the George Eastman House of
Photography on the occasion of the exhibition, "Photography in the
Twentieth Century," which opened at the National Gallery of Canada
in February of 1967. I am indebted to the National Gallery for their
cooperation. I would also like to acknowledge the following: the
Staff of the George Eastman House, with special thanks to Alice
Andrews, Associate Curator, Extension Activities, who acted as my
assistant; Thomas Barrow, Assistant Curator, Extension Activities;
Robert Fichter, Assistant Curator, Exhibitions; Elizabeth Kimbrough,
Assistant Curator, Print Collection; Robert Bretz, Assistant Curator,
Information Center.

The photographs in this book were selected from the extensive print collection of the George Eastman House of Photography. The Museum was chartered by the Regents of the State of New York in 1947. It maintains a permanent collection of photographs, motion pictures, apparatus, documents and books; organizes exhibitions shown in the George Eastman House and circulated throughout the world; conducts research in the history of photography and cinematography; and supports a publications program.

Photography in the Twentieth Century reflects the Museum's responsibility as set forth in its charter, "to establish, develop, and maintain a graphic and continuing history of photography."

introduction

Nathan Lyons
Associate Director and Curator of Photography
The George Eastman House of Photography

This book is primarily intended to provide a visual anthology of the picture making concerns of photographers in the Twentieth Century. Emphasis has been placed upon the development of picture ideas; the challenges, extensions, and restatements of specific points of view.

Photography has represented for many a kind of substitute reality. We view its machine identity, capable of exceptional delineation, as a means for providing literal information about objects and events found in the physical world. Photography confirms for us that these objects or events existed or occurred, and by doing so we have come to accept its basic reality as reality itself.

Any discussion of photography as an expressive medium is usually conditioned by two factors. The first, what the picture should look like and secondly, the subjects it should depict. If photographic statements do not conform to a traditional view of photographic reality, our value judgment carries the essential implication that the pictures must reflect a view of reality which we all hold in common. It appears strange that while photography has contributed so much to extend man's perceptual abilities and thereby his concept of reality, we continue to assess its meaning on somewhat limited terms.

Quite recently Clement Greenberg suggested, "The art in photography is literary art before it is anything else: its triumphs and monuments are historical, anecdotal, reportorial, observational before they are purely pictorial.... The photograph has to tell a story if it is to work as art. And it is in choosing and accosting his story, or subject, that the artist-photographer makes the decisions crucial to his art. Everything else—the pictorial values and the plastic values, the composition and its accents—will more or less derive from these decisions."

A thorough study of the photographs in this book will raise some valid questions with regard to this statement, although one must acknowledge that it is still held as a popular view. The half-truth that the photographer is totally controlled by subject overlooks the important and crucial aspect of the perceptual nature of the selective process involved; a factor which has certainly become of the utmost importance to many contemporary painters and print makers as well. Photography is primarily a means of retaining the impressions that an individual deems significant. A relative factor, this holds true for a "snapshot" as well as the work of many committed photographers motivated by people and places, or exploring pictorial and plastic values. The photograph exists not only as evidence of a given moment of response, as Mr. Greenberg has implied, but becomes a reflection of, or commitment to, a continuity of moments. Awareness and intention on the part of the photographer may provide a basis for evaluation, but to understand his selective process, emphasis must be placed on the relationship of photography to perception and viewed in the context of what Harry Callahan suggested as a measure of creative value, "an individual's whole photographic life from beginning to end, and not only in the value of individual pictures."

These photographs, these "decisions made by the eye," as Cartier-Bresson has termed them, possess an essential value beyond that of a substitute reality. Historically, man has entered into a dialogue with what we term the world. It speaks and acts upon him and he has the option of some action which might be considered his answer. His response will be based upon what terms he has involved himself with in this world and the vocabulary (be it written or visual) which he has at his command. He now has an instrument capable of recording and retaining his responses with unprecedented facility. His camera becomes the biographer of his interaction with the world. As his ideas, attitudes, concerns, and responses develop, then also, as a picture maker, he may convey back to this world or to himself the essential nature of his developed response. He may employ conventional or unconventional means and images. This will depend on whether or not he feels that an appropriate vocabulary exists to convey what it is that concerns him. It will only be a question of time before the meaning of these images, when viewed in the context of his own work and that of other picture makers, will become evident to others.

It should be clearly stated that I am not suggesting the complete abandonment of the realistic picture. What I am suggesting is that by photographic realism have we emphasized too stringently, "speaking likeness," insisting upon honest real-life facts? The question which should arise is whether or not the photograph can become a thing in itself, finding for itself an independent existence which may not necessarily be a direct reflection of a traditionally realistic construct.

plates

1897-1917

□ Denotes Color

FREDERICK H. EVANS ca. 1897

ALFRED STIEGLITZ 1911

CLARENCE H. WHITE 1903

EDWARD STEICHEN 1907

FRANK EUGENE ca. 1908

BARON A. DE MEYER ca. 1907

6

JACK COLLINS ca. 1917

EUGENE ATGET ca. 1910

ARNOLD GENTHE 1906

ADAM CLARK VROMAN 1901

LEWIS W. HINE 1913

PAUL STRAND 1916

ALVIN LANGDON COBURN 1917

1921-1929

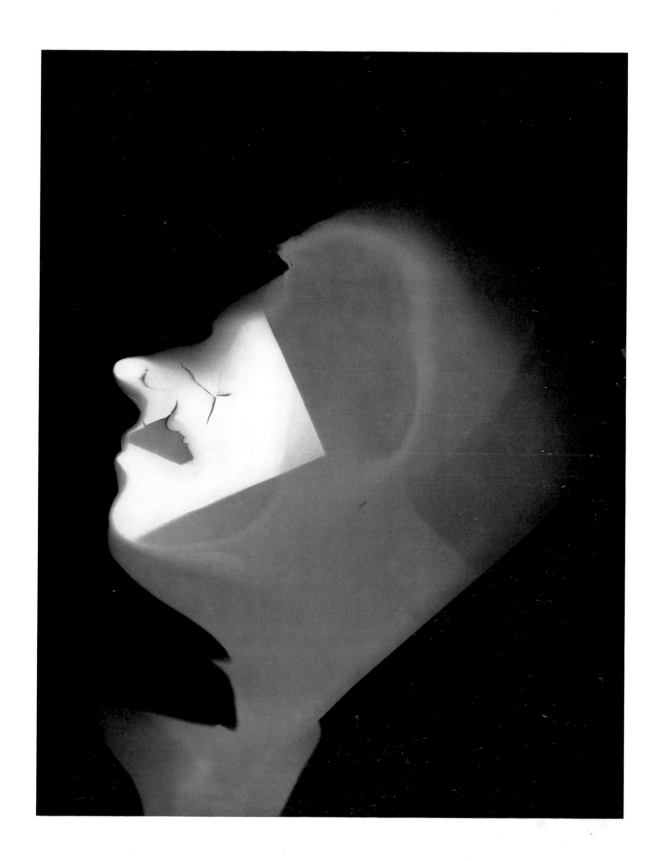

LASZLO MOHOLY-NAGY 1925

ALBERT RENGER-PATZSCH 1922

JOHAN HAGEMEYER 1924

MAN RAY 1921-28

IMOGEN CUNNINGHAM 1929

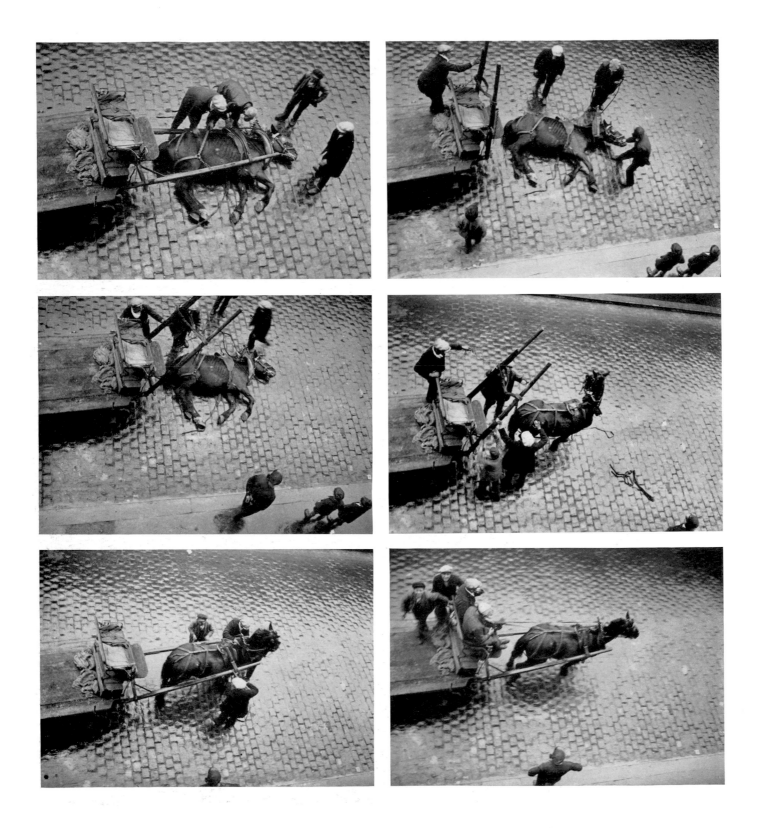

ANDRE KERTESZ 1927

MANUEL ALVAREZ BRAVO   ca. 1929

1930-1949

BERENICE ABBOTT 1930

ERIC SALOMON 1938

BRASSAI ca. 1933

HENRI CARTIER-BRESSON 1932

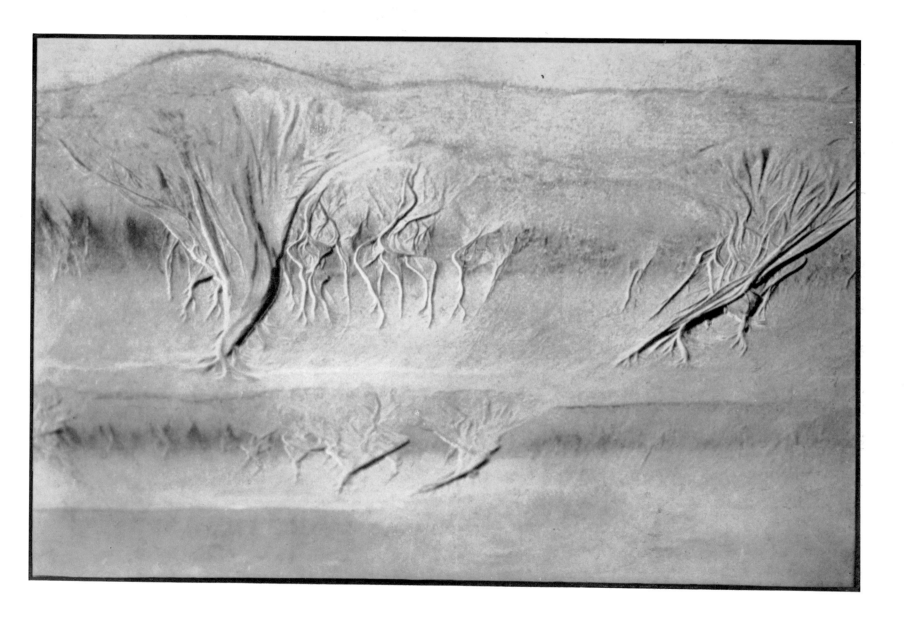

ANNIE W. BRIGMAN 1931

28

WALKER EVANS   1931

DOROTHEA LANGE 1936

ROBERT CAPA 1931

PETER STACKPOLE ca. 1935

GEORGE PLATT LYNES 1931

H. S. WONG 1937

FELIX H. MAN 1931

ARTHUR ROTHSTEIN 1939

MARGARET BOURKE-WHITE 1937

BARBARA MORGAN 1940

VILEM KRIZ ca. 1942

EDWARD WESTON 1940

ARNOLD NEWMAN 1942

ALFRED EISENSTADT 1944

JOE ROSENTHAL 1945

LISETTE MODEL ca. 1942

44

CHARLES ROTKIN ca. 1948

ROSSKAM ca. 1945

SOL LIBSOHN ca. 1945

RUSSELL LEE ca.

GORDON PARKS ca. 1945

TODD WEBB 1948

HELEN LEVITT ca. 1947

WALTER ROSENBLUM 1949

HAROLD CORSINI 1946

FREDERICK SOMMER 1948

PIRKLE JONES 1947

AARON SISKIND 1949

1950-1966

ROBERT FRANK 1955

DAVID DOUGLAS DUNCAN 1950

ROY DE CARAVA ca. 1951

OTTO STEINERT ca. 1950

ANSEL ADAMS 1960

MINOR WHITE 1960

VAL TELBERG 1956-58

W. EUGENE SMITH 1957

TIM KANTOR 1957

WERNER BISCHOF 1954

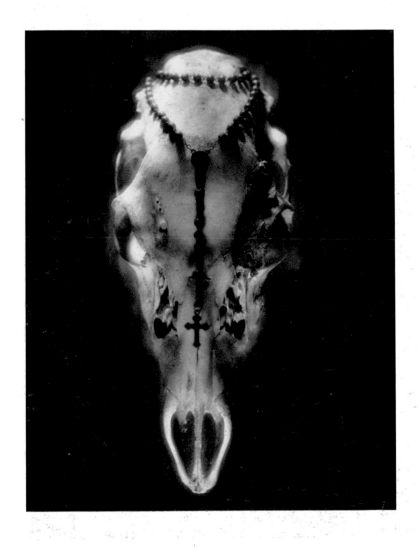

RUTH BERNHARD · 1955

JOHN MAX ca. 1960

WINTER PRATHER 1951

HARRY CALLAHAN 1951

RUTH-MARION BARUCH 1953

BRETT WESTON 1954

WILLIAM GARNETT 1954

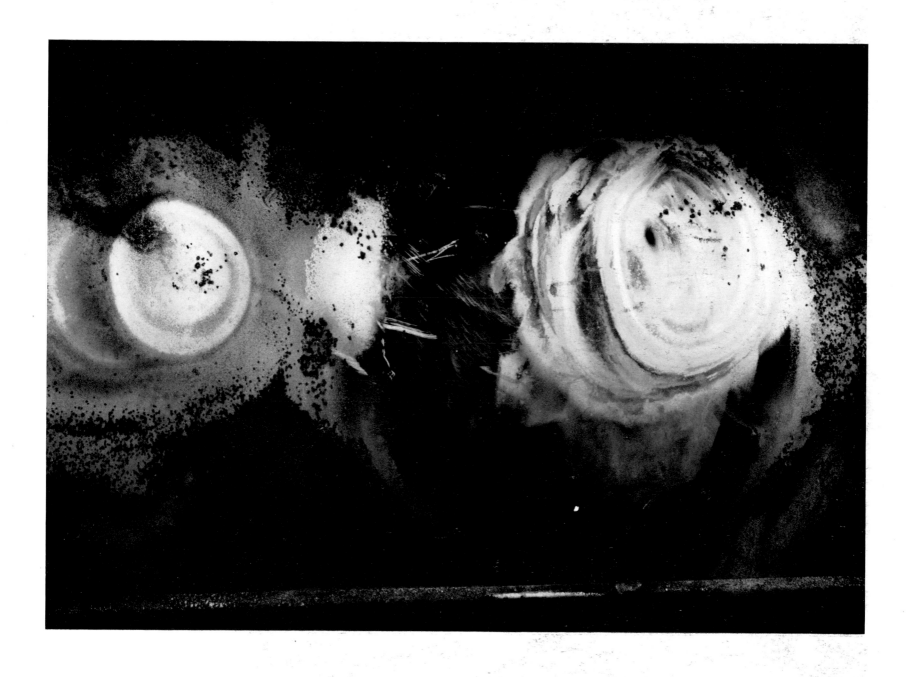

WALTER CHAPPELL 1957

WYNN BULLOCK 1951

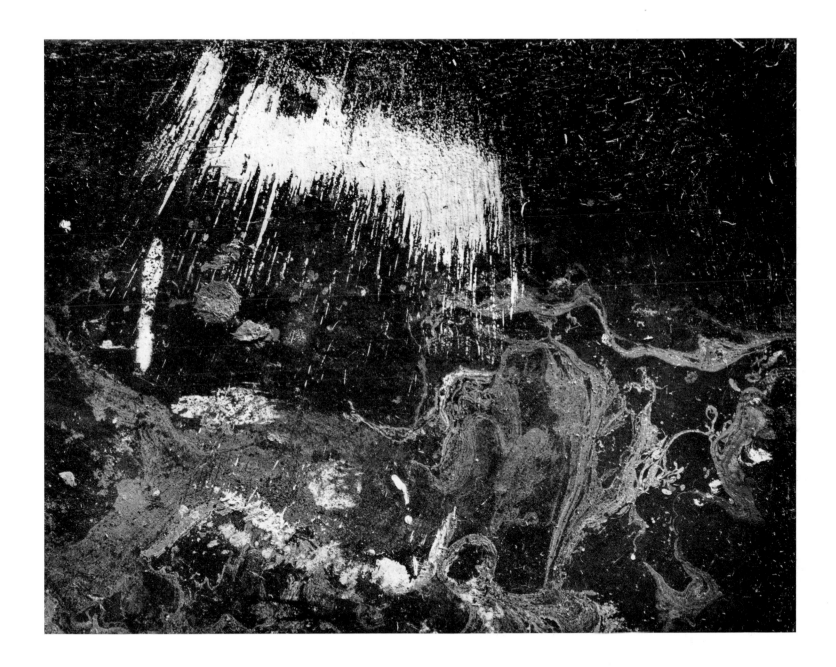

NATHAN LYONS 1959

PAUL CAPONIGRO 1959

SYL LABROT □ ca. 1957

PHILIP HYDE   1956

GERALDINE SHARPE 1962

ERNST HAAS □ 1962

SANNE SANNES 1963

DONALD BLUMBERG 1965

SCOTT HYDE □ 1966

DAVE HEATH 1956

RALPH EUGENE MEATYARD 1962

90

WILLIAM KLEIN 1959

PHILIP JONES GRIFFITHS 1962

KEN HEYMAN 1962

SIMPSON KALISHER 1961

RUDOLPH JANU 1963

JOSEPH STERLING 1961

MARIE COSINDAS 1962

WILLIAM CURRENT 1961

DENNIS STOCK □ 1963

DAN BUDNIK □ 1961

PETE TURNER □ 1961

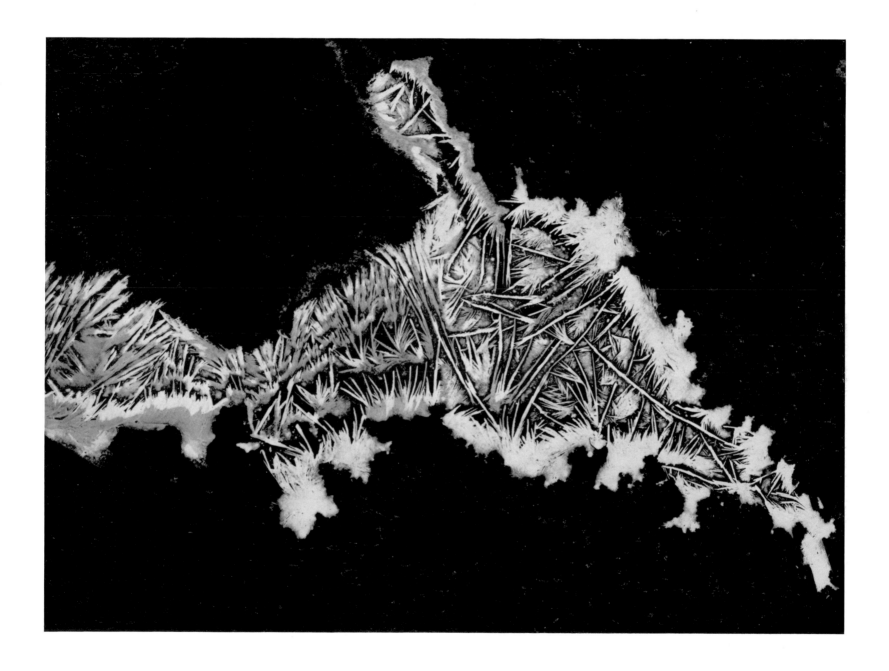

CARL CHIARENZA 1962

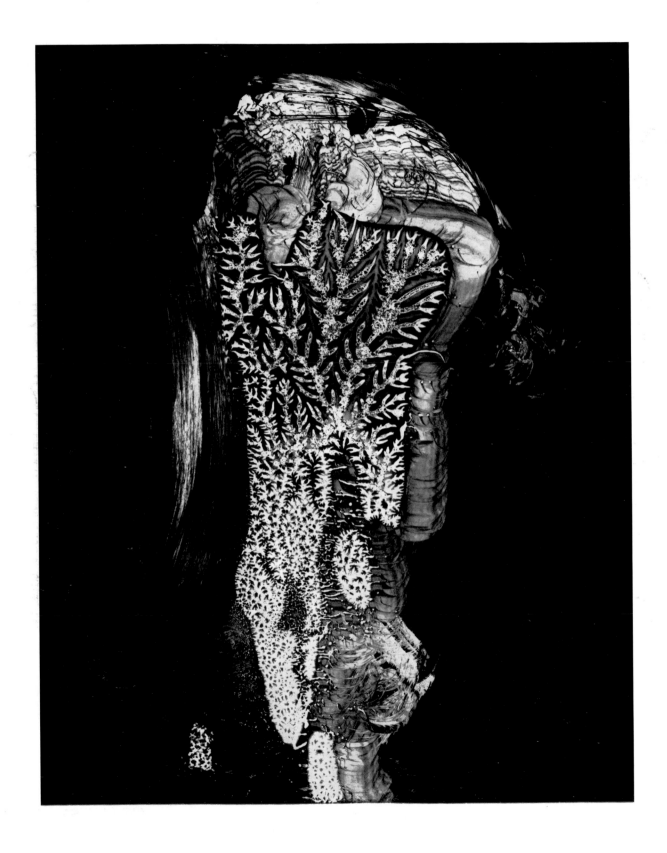

JAMES HILBRANDT 1963

MARIO GIACOMELLI 1965

ROGER MAYNE 1962

CHARLES HARBUTT 1961

EDWARD STURR 1964

OSCAR BAILEY 1960

JAROMIR STEPHANY 1964

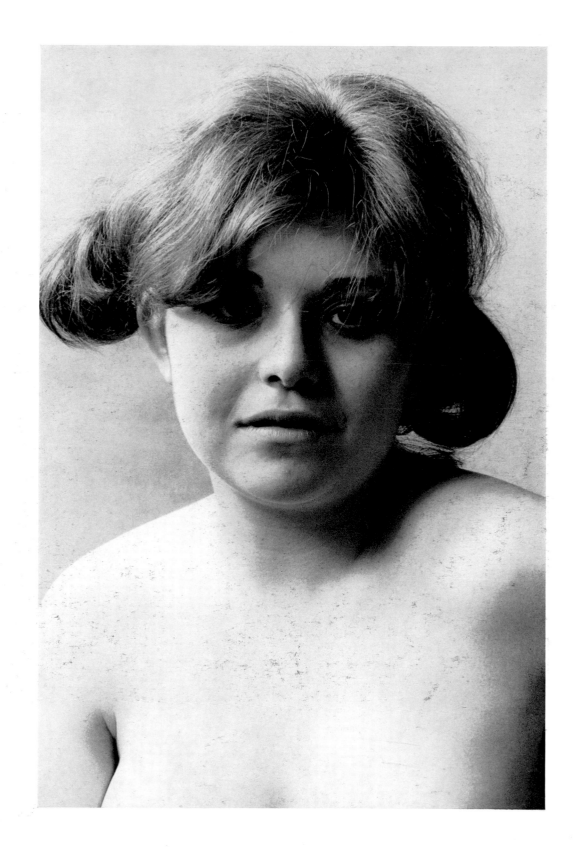

JEAN-LOUIS SWINERS 1963

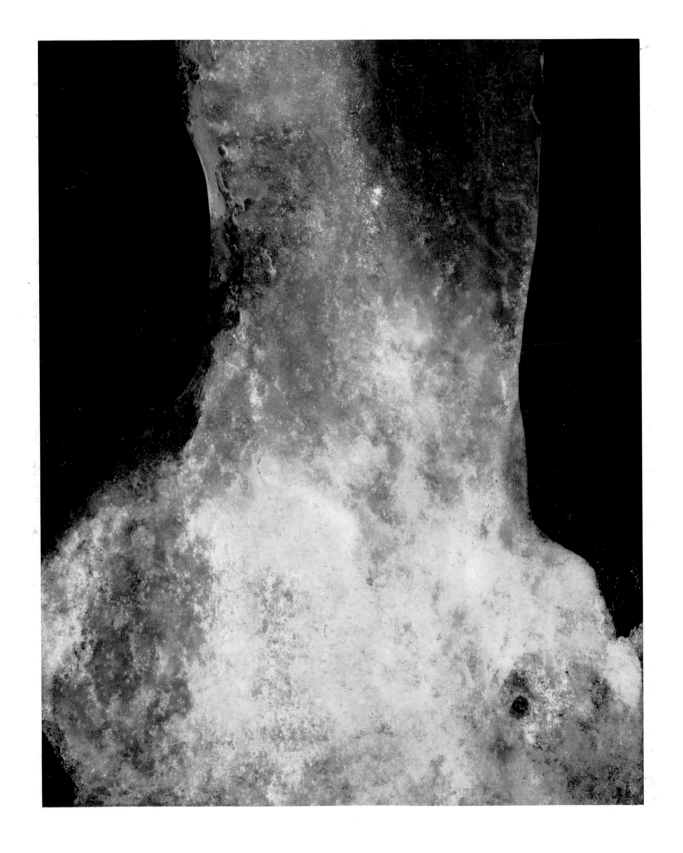

NICHOLAS DEAN 1963

JACK STULER 1963

YASUHIRO ISHIMOTO 1960

JACK WELPOTT 1964

BRUCE DAVIDSON   1958

GARRY WINOGRAND ca. 1960

DUANE MICHALS 1965

ROGER MERTIN 1966

GEORGE KRAUSE 1961

RAY METZKER 1961

ROBERT HEINECKEN □ 1966

NICHOLAS HLOBECZY 1963

ART SINSABAUGH 1961

RICHARD SHORELL 1963

DON NORMARK 1961

ENRICO NATALI   1962-63

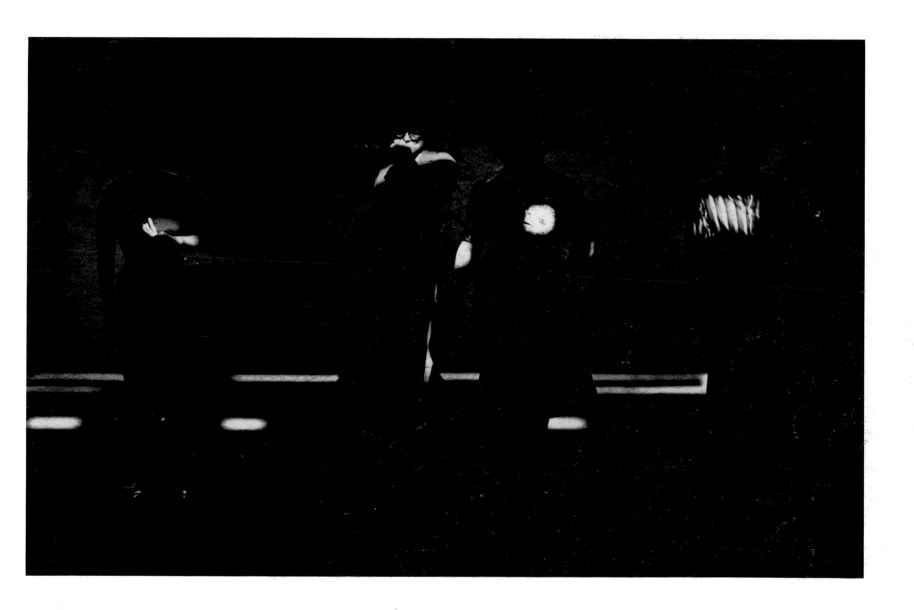

KENNETH JOSEPHSON 1961

EIKOH HOSOE 1963

JOSEPH JACHNA   1964

MICHAEL DI BIASE 1962

DIANE ARBUS 1962

ELLIOT ERWITT ca. 1962

CHARLES SWEDLUND 1963

LEE FRIEDLANDER 1964

FREDERICK BECKMAN 1963

DANNY LYON 1965

JOEL MEYEROWITZ 1965

My Sister Negative and Positive

BETTY HAHN □ 1966